W9-CDY-781

Barbie™

WORD BOOK

DK Publishing, Inc.

LONDON, NEW YORK, MUNICH,
PARIS, MELBOURNE, DELHI

Designer   Ellie Healey
Project Editor and Writer   Fiona Munro
U.S. Editor   Beth Landis
Publishing Manager   Cynthia O'Neill
Art Director   Cathy Tincknell
Production   Nicola Torode

First American Edition, 2001
01 02 03 04 05 10 9 8 7 6 5 4 3 2 1
Published in the United States by DK Publishing, Inc.
95 Madison Avenue New York, NY 10016

BARBIE and associated trademarks are owned by and used under license from Mattel, Inc.
© 2001 Mattel, Inc. All Rights Reserved.

All rights reserved under International and Pan-American Copyright Conventions.
No part of this publication may be reproduced, stored in a retrieval
system, or transmitted in any form or by any means, electronic, mechanical, photocopying,
recording, or otherwise, without prior written permission of the copyright owner.
Published in Great Britain by Dorling Kindersley Limited.

Library of Congress Cataloging-in-Publication Data
Barbie word book.-- 1st American ed.
    p. cm.
  ISBN 0-7894-7336-4
  1. Vocabulary--Juvenile literature. 2. Barbie dolls--Juvenile literature. [1. Vocabulary.]
  I. Dorling Kindersley Publishing, Inc.

PE1449 .B+
428.I–dc21

        2001028435

Reproduced by Media Development
Printed and bound in China by L. Rex

Acknowledgments
Barbie® doll photography by Lee Katz, Shirley Ushirogata, Greg Roccia,
Ali Farboud, Lisa Collins, Judy Tsuno, and the Mattel Photo Studio

Additional photography by Trish Gant and © Dorling Kindersley.
For further information see: www.dkimages.com

Dorling Kindersley would like to thank the following for their kind permission to reproduce their images:
Balloon Base, p23, right center.

The publisher would also like to thank:
The staff at Mattel, Inc., especially Monica Lopez, Vicki Jaeger, Lisa Collins, and Judy Tsuno.

see our complete catalog at
www.dk.com

Barbie™ WORD BOOK

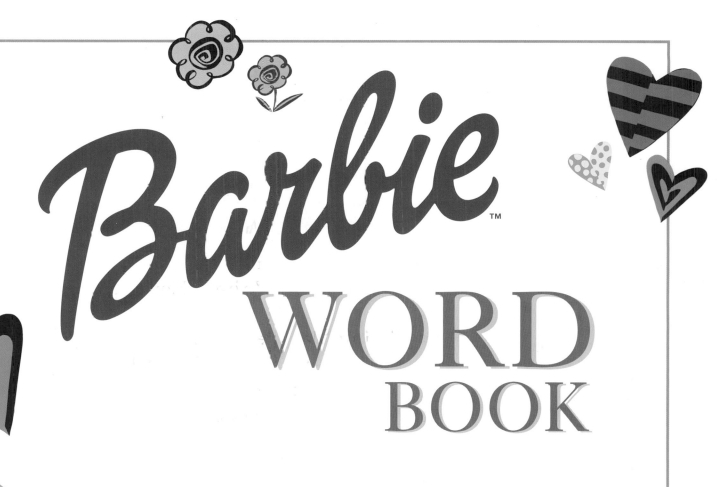

Hi, everyone!

The *Barbie Word Book* is designed to help your child take the first steps toward learning to read. It's packed with specially photographed scenes showing Barbie and her friends, as well as colorful photographs of everyday objects.

Each bright page introduces children to useful new words, and you can help build their vocabulary by talking about what you see in each picture. Encourage children to use their new vocabulary to describe what Barbie is doing.

Every page features clearly labeled photos of everyday things. To connect words and images in your child's mind, point to the pictures as you read the labels. This is one of the first and most important steps in learning to read. There are over 300 pictures to find, say, and spell throughout the book.

The beautiful photographs, packed with detail, make this book one that Barbie fans will want to return to again and again, increasing their word and observation skills along the way.

Learning is so much fun with Barbie!

At Home

Can you spot the objects around the edge of the page in this picture of me in my family room? Which of these things do you have in your home?

window

stereo

door

mug

gate

picture

sofa

lamp

potted plant

cabinet

cushion

floor

rug

television

bookshelf

table

telephone

armchair

Colors and Shapes

Can you spot the colors found around the edge in the main picture? How many different shapes can you see? Point to them as you find them.

purple

oval

gray

square

brown

diamond

black

red

circle

blue

heart

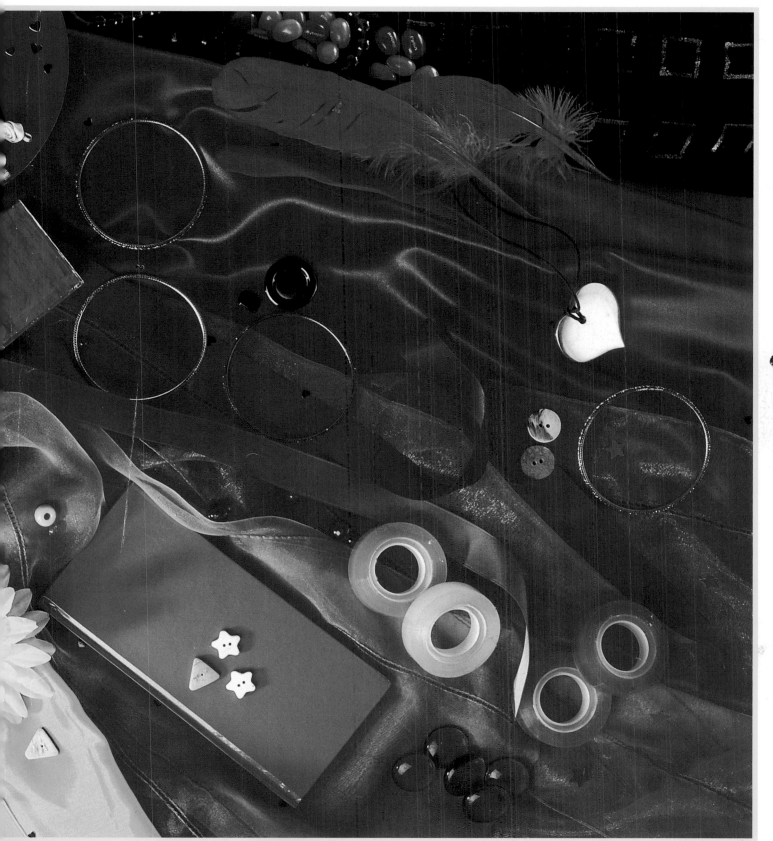

yellow

star

green

triangle

pink

rectangle

orange

Cover Girl

I love to wear cool clothes! Can you spot and say the different clothes and other objects in this busy studio? What do you like to wear?

jeans

dress

hanger

cardigan

hat

camera

shoes

t-shirt

pants

scarf

jacket

sneakers

skirt

clothes
rack

purse

necklace

baseball cap

photograph

pocket

sandals

Opposites

Big is the opposite of small, and long is the opposite of short. Point to the other opposites around the edge and find them in the picture.

open

closed

curly

straight

hard

soft

rough

light

heavy

front

back

short

long

dry

wet

new

smooth

thick

thin

big

small

old

What's Cooking?

I love to cook, and my kitchen is full of delicious treats! Can you see your favorite thing to eat in the picture? What can I make for brunch today?

knife

spoon

fork

dish towel

oven mitt

bowl

bread

glass

frying pan

cereal

milk

grocery bag

butter

turkey

flour

olive oil

pasta

juice

jelly

cheese

tea kettle

eggs

cake

Hobby Time

Here are some things people use to enjoy sports and hobbies. Do you have any pastimes? What do you like to do best?

recorder

ice skate

goggles

tennis ball

jump rope

whistle

ballet slipper

tennis racket

pom-pom

guitar

basketball

tambourine

compact disc

riding helmet

photo album

sketch book

Beach Time

We're having fun on our vacation! The summer sun is shining in a bright blue sky, and we're wakeboarding on the ocean. It's beautiful at the beach!

palm tree

umbrella

sand

sun

shells

wakeboard

pearl

starfish

beach ball

swimsuit

seaweed

sandcastle

shovel

bucket

crab

dolphin

seagulls

waves

mermaid

Fruits and Vegetables

Look at all the fruits and vegetables in this beautiful picture. Which ones do you like to eat? What is your favorite fruit?

blueberry

lime

watermelon

cucumber

pear

pea

spinach

carrot

potato

tomato

apple

pineapple

kiwi fruit

banana

cauliflower

pepper

strawberry

onion

broccoli

grape

sweetcorn

peach

eggplant

string bean

orange

School Days

Today I am helping out at Kelly's kindergarten. Take a look around! There are lots of things for you to spy in the classroom. Can you say the alphabet?

teacher

chair

beanbag chairs

chalk

alphabet

blackboard

numbers

books

playhouse

clock

globe

pen

pencil

paper

paint

toy box

Getting Around

There are so many different ways of getting around. Find the things around the edge of the page on my bulletin board.

baby carriage

truck

skateboard

ambulance

THIS WEEK'S DELIVERY WILL BE ON TUESDAY AT 10:30AM

Baby

For.......
On.......
At.......

date ....
time ....

HELICOPTER HEAVE

PARTY

Sponsored Bike Ride

Name	Amount per mile	Total

Help raise $5,000 for the City Hospital

SCOOTER RALLY

Come along on your scooter and join in the fun!

Starts Saturday at 10am in the park

Bob Boat R

Dinghys
Sailing Boa
Catamaran
Life Preserv
Wet suits

PLANE TICKETS

F.M. AIRLINES

COOL CARS

beach buggy

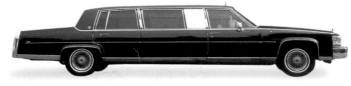

limousine

helicopter

scooter

boat

in-line skate

motorcycle

bicycle

car

balloon

bus

TRAIN TRAVEL

Red Line

1 ADULT
TICKET
NO. 01754

Can't wait to show you my
new bike!

YELLOW TAXIS

A Smoother Ride

CITY HOSPITAL
Volunteer ID: 306
Name: Barbie

Ken

Cool Moves

moving services

Saturday night
Drive - Thru

Saturday

taxi

airplane

train

Picnic at the Park

There are lots of things to spot and say on a picnic in the park — some are big and some are tiny. Can you spot them all?

bushes

grass

flowerbed

ball

caterpillar

ladybug

butterfly

seesaw

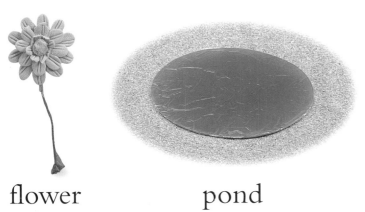
flower

pond

picnic basket

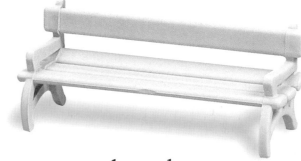
bench

kite

clouds

slide

birds

swings

duck

blanket

Storytime

My little sister is learning to read, and I love to read with her at bedtime. Can you spot all the special storytime words in the picture?

wizard

knight

jester

castle

dragon

black cat

magic wand

beanstalk

goose

fairy

broomstick

robe

crown

king

queen

prince

golden egg

sword

pumpkin

rainbow

princess

Pet Hospital

Stacie is helping out at the pet hospital today. Veterinarian Barbie is checking a cat who has just had kittens! What else can you see at the hospital?

veterinarian

pet carrier

fish tank

bandage

turtle

leash

paws

dog

dog biscuits

cat

collar

goldfish

kitten

rabbit

puppy

dog bowl

gerbils

pet medicine

Sleepover

It's so much fun when friends stay over at my house. We love to read magazines and chat until it's time for bed.

bedding

pajamas

faucet

hairdryer

comb

soap

bubble bath

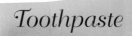
toothpaste

pillow

bed

hairbrush

bath robe

bathtub

mirror

teddy bear

toothbrush

washcloth

shampoo

towel

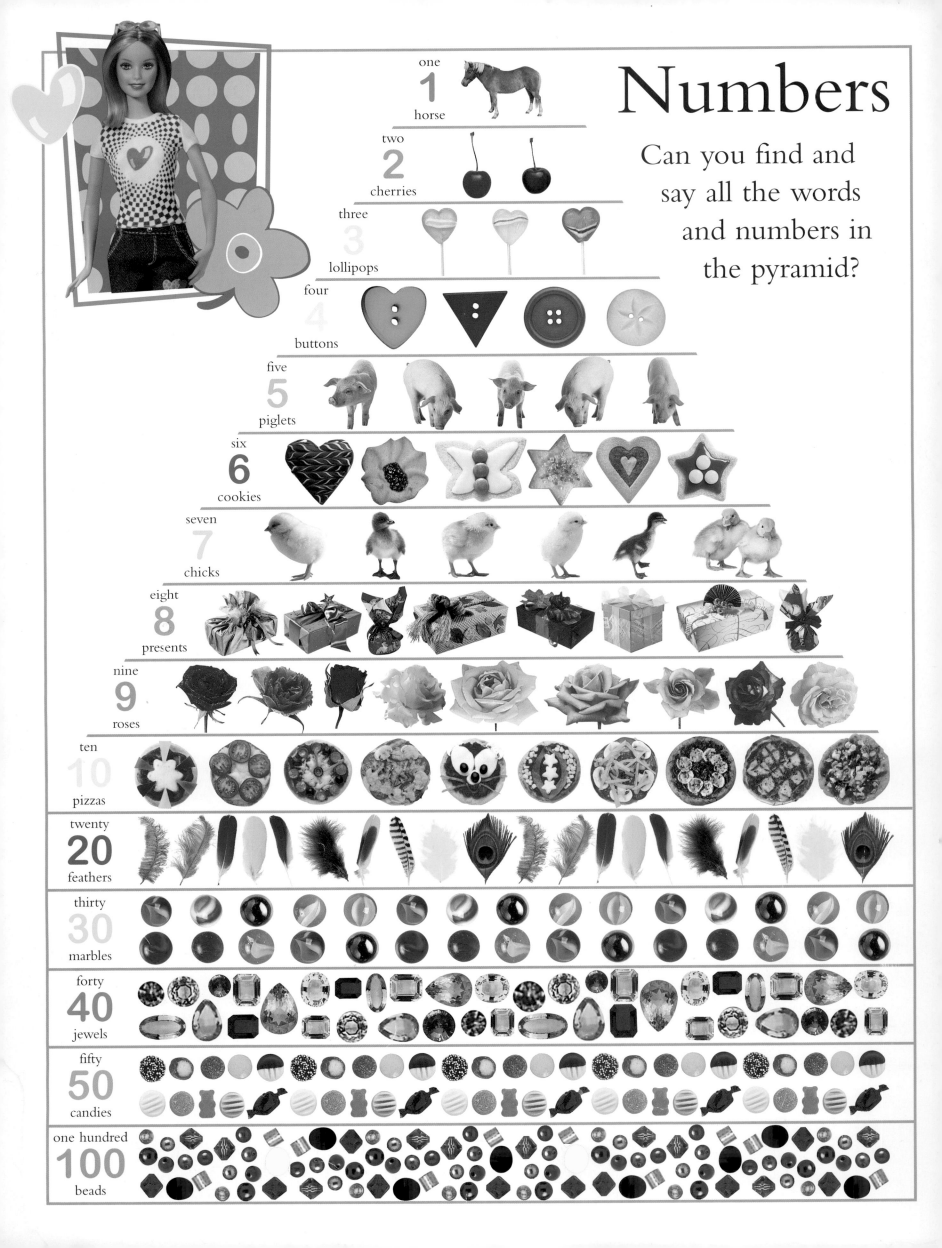

Numbers

Can you find and say all the words and numbers in the pyramid?

one
1
horse

two
2
cherries

three
3
lollipops

four
4
buttons

five
5
piglets

six
6
cookies

seven
7
chicks

eight
8
presents

nine
9
roses

ten
10
pizzas

twenty
20
feathers

thirty
30
marbles

forty
40
jewels

fifty
50
candies

one hundred
100
beads